MODELLER'S GUIDE TO

MOULD MAKING AND RESIN CASTING

MODELLER'S GUIDE TO

MOULD MAKING AND RESIN CASTING

ALEX HORNOR

First published in Great Britain by Swordworks Books

ISBN 978-1-906512-57-6

Printed and bound in the UK & US

A catalogue record of this book is available from the British Library

Cover design by Swordworks Books

CONTENTS

FOREWORD

Making models by using the skills of mouldmaking and casting is a hobby that is becoming increasingly popular. Finding the correct manual to guide you through the process is not always easy, and we have attempted here to pull as many threads together as possible to give you the clearest possible insight and knowledge into duplicating small or even large models using mouldmaking and casting techniques.

The object you wish to duplicate is known as a pattern, this model is a 3-dimensional object you use as the pattern to make a mould from. You do not need specialized equipment make moulds and carry out basic casting operations.

Everything starts, however, from a drawing or

3-dimensional object created by sculpting, carving, construction, and so on.

We wish to the greatest of enjoyment with your new hobby.

INTRODUCTION

Mouldmaking and casting is an old process, dating back as far as 3000 years. Despite the availability of new equipment and materials, the essential basics of mouldmaking and casting have not really changed since then. For the model maker, it is a very useful, if not essential skill to master. Sometimes parts need to be fabricated in small quantities, sometimes in larger quantities. Modelling once really attractive figure is a lengthy process (unless using CNC equipment) but very rewarding. Being called up on to produce further batches of the same model would be very arduous, hence the value of duplicating it through mouldmaking and casting.

Moulding or moulding is the process of

manufacturing by shaping pliable raw material using a model called a pattern. A mould or mould is a hollowed-out block that is filled with a liquid or uncured material. The liquid hardens or sets inside the mould, adopting its shape. A mould is the opposite of a cast. The manufacturer who makes the moulds is called the mouldmaker. A release agent is typically used to make removal of the hardened/ set substance from the mould easier. Common mouldmaking materials are latex, which is cheap and easy to use, and RTV, which is more expensive but makes a much stronger mould that will stand higher temperatures if the modeller wishes to use low temperature metals.

Casting is the process where liquid material, often polyester resin, is poured into a mould, which has a cavity of the desired shape, and then allowed to solidify. The solidified part is also known as a casting, which is removed from the mould to complete the process. Casting materials may be plaster, resin, which is a 2 part mixture that cures within the mould and low temperature metals. Casting is most often used for making models such as military miniatures and vehicle models that would be otherwise difficult to make by other methods.

CHAPTER 1

OVERVIEW OF MOULDMAKING AND CASTING

Before we delve into the technical aspects of making the perfect mould, then using it to cast the perfect model, or model part, we need to describe exactly what is each individual part of the process. Later we will examine each step and show in straightforward detail how to carry out the mould making and casting processes to produce perfect results from the word go.

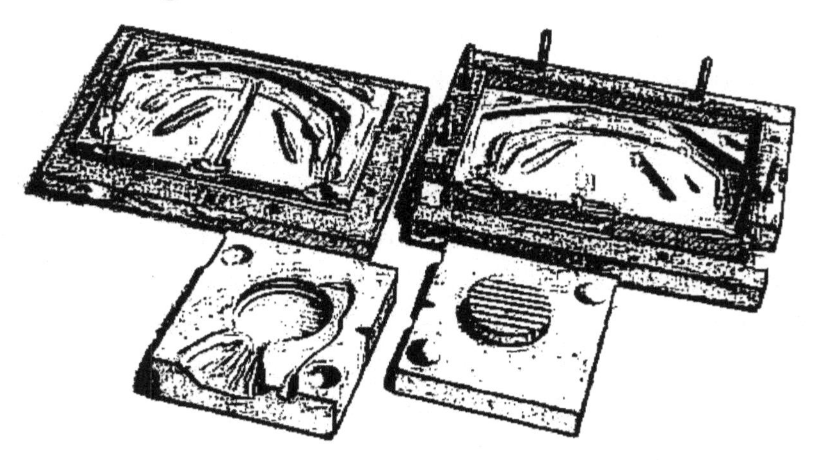

Before beginning to make the mould, it is of course necessary to have an object that you wish to make or copy. If you are making, for example, a prototype of a part or artefact, perhaps a military miniature, you need to create the former, or plug, from which to make your mould. This can be done by hand, using techniques such as sculpting, carving and possibly using a similar object which you can modify to make the object you require. Using the military miniature as an example, if you have an infantryman from Wellington's army at Waterloo, it should be possible, with care, to remove some parts of the model, add others and perhaps modify others, to produce one of Napoleon's infantrymen of the same period.

The other way to make the original object from a 3d drawing is to use a CNC milling machine, which will produce a virtually finished model from which you can make a mould and produce many more of the same model. There are also specialised pieces of equipment called rapid prototyping machines that are able to take CAD drawings and create a mould or a part directly from a 3D drawing, this is not yet something that many home craftsperson would find affordable although increasing numbers of modellers are finding the cost of CNC milling machines to have dropped considerably, to the point that they are much more affordable.

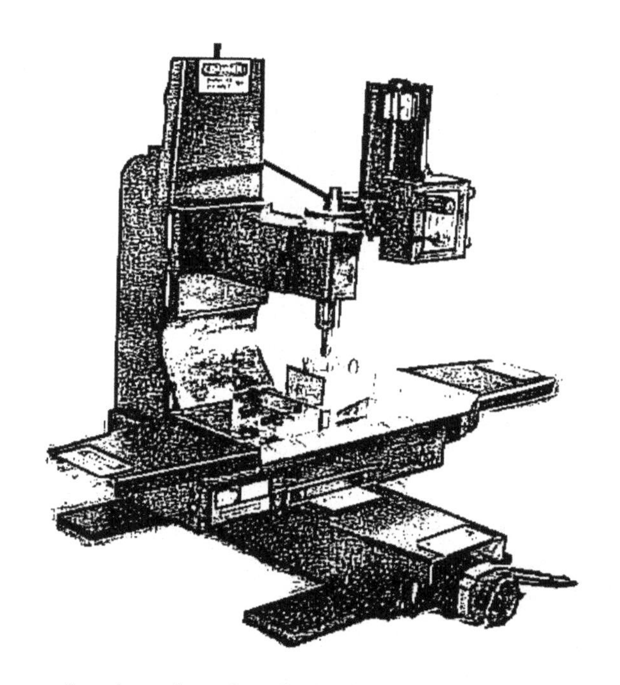

Bench top Low Cost CNC Milling Machine

Once we have the object to be copied, the next step is to make the mould. A mould is something that will shape the casting material into an exact copy of the object from which the mould was made. The casting material itself can be resin, normally used for a wide range of models, often reinforced and enhanced with the addition of metal particles to give the finished product the appearance and weight of a model made completely of metal, such as a bronze statuette.

Cast Resin Military Miniature

If you use modern rubber materials, mouldmaking is usually quite easy. The easiest type of mould to make is for an object like a plaque. You can just put the plaque in a box, pour rubber mouldmaking material over it, let the rubber cure, and you're done. With new clear rubber materials, you can even make moulds of very complicated objects in the same way - by putting the object in a container, and covering it with the clear rubber. Once the rubber cures, you can cut the rubber into two or more pieces to release the pattern.

Latex is a commonly used material for making moulds. It is relatively cheap and easy to use. Latex derives from the rubber tree and is vulcanised with sulphur to form a liquid milky white substance. The Latex product is used extensively in the mould making industry where removal of the mould from the master is done by stretching it. The Latex mould can then later be filled and cast with resin, plaster and other normally cold casting materials.

Pouring Latex

In most cases Latex is safe to use. It is especially used in the production of babies "dummies", balloons, gloves, condoms etc. Some people can be allergic to latex and should use a protective barrier cream when handling. In some rare instances this can be serious. If in doubt, you should take steps to protect yourself from potential latex allergy.

Treat latex as a paint. Use an old paint brush and paint it directly on to the master allowing one or two minutes between coats to dry. You may find it best to use latex in a warm dry room where such ideal atmospheric conditions would aid the drying process. In addition to using a paint brush, after the initial coat as been applied, you can save time by dipping the master into latex directly.

Using traditional mouldmaking methods, with materials such as plaster, it can be very difficult and time consuming for certain more complex shapes. If you make plaster moulds of rigid objects, for instance, you may need to make the mould in many different pieces so that you can get the plaster off the model.

The materials and techniques for mouldmaking and casting do not require a lot of space or special equipment. Making moulds and castings for personal use, such as for your hobbies, can be done on a kitchen tabletop or bench in your workshop. For most projects, the only equipment you need is disposable mixing bowls and mixing sticks. For some casting materials, such as plastic resins, you should do your mixing out-of-doors in fresh air or ensure that you have professional ventilation in your work area as well as protective masks for all people involved in the process. It is best to mix plaster and concrete in the open air and this process can generate a great deal of dust.

If you get into making larger items such as

concrete moulds and concrete castings, you will probably want a larger workspace such as a carport or garage. For casting ceramics, you need a kiln, a double boiler if you want to make candles, a simple electric melting pot if you want to cast low-melting temperature metals; and a cheap glass microwave dish if you want to work with hot melt vinyl.

Concrete is something made by mixing cement with aggregates such as sand and gravel and adding water. Cement can be bought in sack, as can sand, and gravel. You then mix your own concrete. Or you can buy a sack of ready-mixed concrete, which has all the dry ingredients so that you can just add water. It is common to use the terms cement and concrete to mean the same thing.

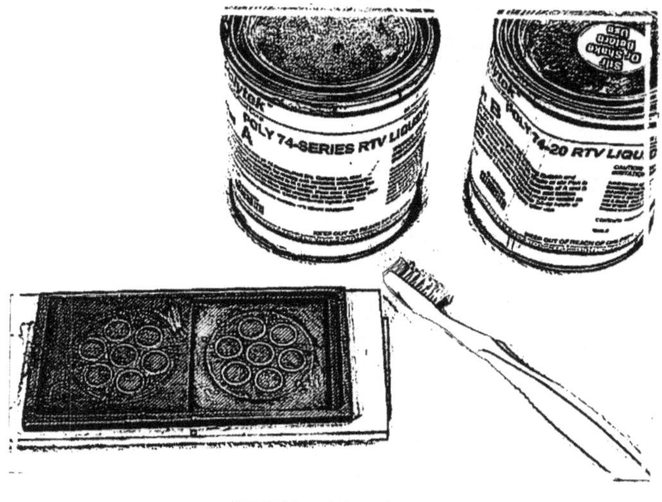

RTV Mouldmaking

Plastic resins are usually used with various types of fillers. The fillers make the cured resin stronger, save cost because less resin is used, and impart a desired look to the cured plastic.

Pecan resin is plastic resin in which very finely ground up pecan shells ("pecan flour") has been used as filler. The pecan flour is the same consistency as ordinary baking flour. Cured pecan resin has a look similar to walnut wood. Porcelain resin is plastic resin in which powdered clay has been used as a filler to make imitation porcelain. Aluminium Trihydrate can also be used for a more translucent look. Cultured marble is plastic resin in which calcium carbonate (also called marble dust) has been used as filler. In addition to fillers, colours can also be added to plastic resins to further enhance the look. Various pigments are almost always added to cultured marble resins to give a natural "streaks-of-colour" look.

Many terms have been created for plastic resin castings in an attempt to make them seem more desirable. All the terms refer to the same basic thing, plastic resin with some type of filler in it. Cold-cast resin, cold-cast bronze, imitation stone, marble resin, indoor/outdoor resin, cast marble and bonded marble are all commonly used terms to describe resin mixed with an additional substance to enhance it.

If you wish, it is possible to make resin castings that resemble foam castings. To actually cast foam is an expensive operation, but you can easily make plastic resin castings that have many of the same qualities as foam, but are not actually foam. You need extremely lightweight fillers in the plastic resin to make very lightweight but durable products. For such things as duck decoys, taxidermy mounts and fishing lures these techniques are ideal.

Spin Casting Machine

A popular casting material with military modellers is low melting temperature metal, such as lead, tin, pewter and similar alloys. This type of metal casting is straightforward and requires a minimum of casting equipment and safety equipment. Other types of metal casting, including brass, bronze, aluminium, gold, silver, and cast iron, require very different materials and techniques and much more in the way of equipment, space, and safety precautions, due to the very high heat levels required to melt these materials.

If you make a mould from a flexible material such as latex rubber, it may distort out of shape when you put a casting material into it. For this reason it is sometimes necessary to make a separate support to hold the mould, otherwise when a large quantity of casting material is poured into it, it can distort badly out of shape. We shall describe later how to make these specialist supports.

Release Agent

Release agents are often essential for casting your objects, they are a substance that prevents one material from sticking to another. When you make moulds or castings, release agents may not be necessary, or they may be merely helpful, or they may be absolutely necessary.

Originally, rubber had to be vulcanized, a combination of heat and pressure, to make it into a permanent rubber mould.

Without vulcanization, the rubber would stay sticky or gummy and would not be durable. Certain types of rubber still used today need to be vulcanized also. Those rubbers are usually used for industrial applications or where the rubber is going to be exposed to high temperatures.

Modern mould making rubber used by modellers today is RTV. RTV stands for "Room Temperature Vulcanizing" and refers to a rubber material that cures completely at room temperature. This type of rubber is the most common for making poured moulds. After you mix the rubber and pour it over your model, it sets up at room temperature, without needing any sort of heat treatment.

Examples of RTV rubber are polyurethane rubber and silicone rubber. RTV is a two mix that sets chemically to form a hard rubber mould.

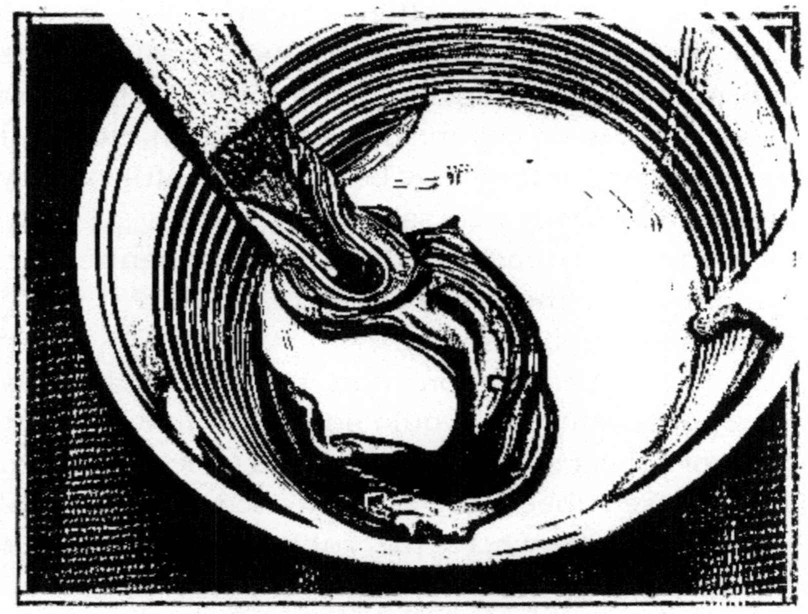

Gently stirring RTV 2 part mix

RTV comes in the base plus curative; A+B) available in a hardness range of very soft to medium. They are available for making moulds that are poured, brushed or sprayed on to a model and have performance characteristics that no other mould rubber has. RTV rubber has the best release properties of all the mould rubbers, which is especially an advantage when doing production casting of resins, polyurethanes, polyesters and epoxy. Sometimes, no release agent is required, so there is no post-production cleanup. Silicones also exhibit very good chemical resistance and high temperature resistance, 400°F / 205°C and higher. High temperature resistance makes silicone the only mould rubber suitable for casting low melt metal alloys, tin, pewter, lead. The combination of good release properties, chemical resistance and heat resistance makes silicone the best choice for production casting of resins.

It is also possible to make moulds out of a plastic/ rubber composition, that goes liquid when heated, then solid when it cools. This material can be reheated and therefore re-used a number of times, making it suitable for a range of casting materials. It is not suitable to hot casting, as the very property that makes it re-usable will also cause it to melt.

We will go through the various mouldmaking and casting techniques step by step later in this book and explore how to use the correct technique for your project.

CHAPTER 2

STARTING MOULDMAKING

An original plug is the first requirement, from which to make the mould. It can be made from wood coated with polyester or epoxy resin. It can also be made of plaster, RTV silicone or foam. Your choice of plug-making material is limited only by your imagination. Plaster, foams and low density materials seldom last more than one mould. If several moulds are to be pulled from the plug, a polyester and fibreglass plug can be used to make several moulds.

The plug should be glossy and as defect-free as possible to minimize the amount of sanding and buffing of the mould. If the mould requires some cosmetic reworking, care must be taken to avoid changing its dimensions or features.

Once the project has been chosen and a suitable model or other artefact is ready to be moulded and cast, the next step is to prepare the mould. As stated in the previous chapter, some moulds, especially latex moulds, do require additional support so that the weight of the resin or other casting material does not distort the mould rubber and ruin the cast object. This rarely applies to RTV moulds, of course, as these moulds, made from a fairly rigid 2 part mix, tend to be strong enough to support most casting materials. The only exception fort RTV moulds would be in the case of larger moulds or for more awkward shapes.

Simple Mould Box

Let's look at making a mould box. A mould box does not have to be a complex structure. Depending on the size and configuration of your model, often a small saucepan or similar container, perhaps even a biscuit tin, may be sufficient. If you make moulds of flat - two dimensional models on a regular basis and require a mould box there are a number of advantages in constructing your own mould box.

A mould box is easy to construct and requires minimal assembly. It is certainly reusable and in most cases will be adjustable for different sizes of mould and model.

To accommodate the model, use retaining walls made of ½" (1.3 cm) thick acrylic strips. We selected acrylic because most mould rubbers release easily from acrylic. Wood can also be used. Four pieces are cut for the shorter side of the retaining wall and four pieces were cut for the longer side of the retaining wall. These pieces are then assembled together in an "L" shape with screws.

Secure the model to the baseboard, which should be at least twice the size of the original model to allow enough working space. Secure the model to the backboard by applying a bead of hot melt glue around the perimeter of the reverse side of the model. Press model firmly onto baseboard and create a tight seal where the model meets the baseboard. This will prevent liquid rubber from leaking underneath the model.

Now assemble the retaining walls around the model. Place retaining pieces around the model, making certain there is slight gap between the cameo and retaining wall. This gap will equal the wall thickness of the cured rubber mould.

Fasten the retaining walls together with C-clamps and apply hot melt glue to any seams where the liquid rubber may leak out. This includes seams where the retaining walls meet the baseboard and also where retaining walls meet one another.

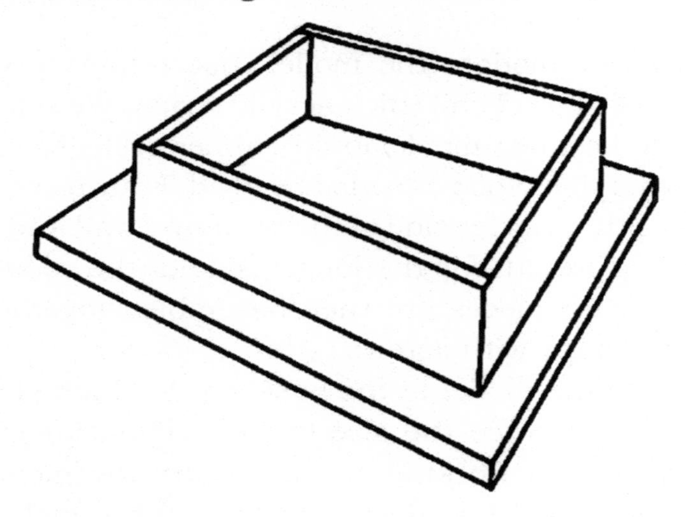

Mould Box built for specific purpose

Once you have your object prepared to be moulded, and a suitably sized moulding box built, if necessary, the next step is to consider which mouldmaking medium you wish to use. Some materials are ideal for one purpose, but not for others. Latex, the first of our materials to be considered, it ideal in many respects to begin with. It is cheap to buy and relatively easy to use, making it an ideal medium to begin.

A word of warning: Latex is NOT suitable for casting hot materials, pewter, white metal etc. For this type of material, RTV, which we cover later, is ideal.

MOULDMAKING WITH LATEX.

Latex rubber is a natural material, obtained from a species of tropical tree. It is compounded in various ways to make liquids suitable for moulding, casting, dipping, and making foam rubber. Latex rubber for making moulds is a thick liquid or paste. You can use it to make a thin mould of a model by brushing on or dipping on several coats. When the coats are dry and cured, the result is an extremely elastic and strong rubber mould. Since the mould is so thin, you may need to make a backup mould from plaster or fibreglass for support. You should note that latex is very useful for making moulds of models with severe undercuts.

Note in the picture of the Abraham Lincoln the severe undercuts present in the model, especially beneath the president's shoulders. These can present problems to the mouldmaker, latex is one product that will make mouldmaking and casting more straightforward for this type of artefact. Because this could well be a larger, more awkwardly shaped model, it is likely that a mould box will be necessary.

Abraham Lincoln bust cast out of latex mould

SAFETY

Keep out of the reach of children. The latex contains ammonia. Use with adequate ventilation. Do not breathe fumes directly over an open container. Keep container covered when not in use, and between dipping a model or coating your brush. In case of skin contact, wash with soap and water. Wear rubber gloves if your skin is sensitive to this material. Wear eye protection. In case of contact, flush with water for 15 minutes and see a doctor if necessary. Always read and follow the manufacturer's safety recommendations.

To begin making latex moulds, you will need the following equipment:

- Liquid soap.
- Disposable artist's type brushes.
- Plastic or glass containers with lids.
- Talcum Powder
- Oven or hair dryer.

If you plan to make latex moulds out of copper and manganese models, you should know that latex is very sensitive to materials containing these materials. They will cause the latex and moulds made from the latex to discolour and degrade. Do not use any containers or stirring rods made from copper, brass, or bronze.

Materials for Resin Casting

Latex may stick to your model unless you use a release agent. An inexpensive release agent is petroleum jelly, also known as Vaseline. Use a very thin coat. You can also use wax polish, such as ordinary neutral shoe polish. A lot of petroleum products, solvents, and oils are not compatible with latex and will cause degradation of the rubber.

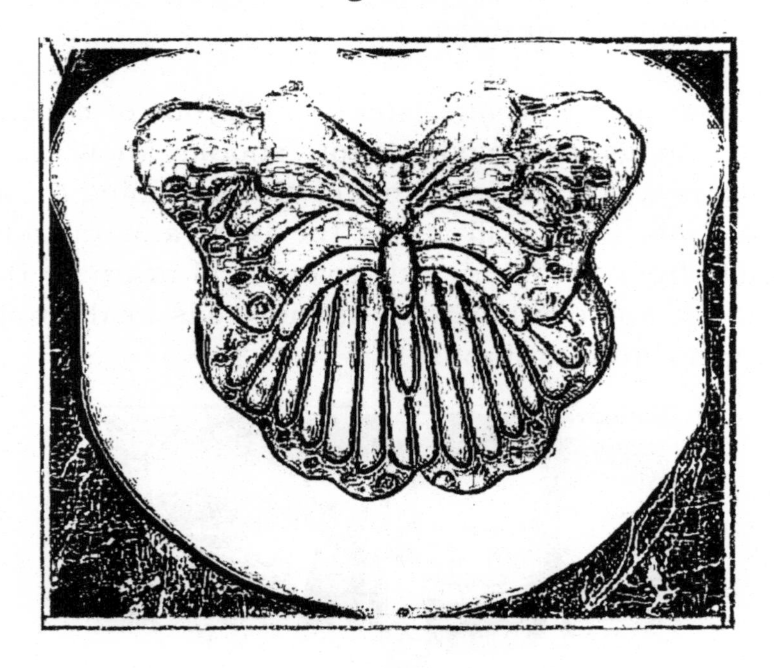

Latex Mould

Models made from plaster, wax, glazed ceramic, or glass do not normally require a release agent. You should coat some types of Oil Base Clay with release agent so the oils in the clay do not affect the rubber. Water Base Clay does not need a release if it is still damp, but will if it is dry.

Removing latex mould from model

You must ensure that you seal porous models, such as models made from wood, plaster and other similarly porous materials, with several coats of lacquer or varnish. Moulding rubber will seep into unsealed wood and lock into the pores. This will make removal of the mould difficult or impossible. You should use a release agent over the sealed model.

When preparing the latex, you should mix it by stirring slowly until the latex is an even, creamy consistency. Try not to generate any air bubbles. Every time you open the bottle or other container of latex a small amount of water will evaporate from the latex, especially around the lid and container threads. The latex in these areas will coagulate into rubber. Do not try to mix coagulated rubber back into the latex. If the rubber gets in your way you can peel it off and discard it. Keep the container closed when not in use, even if only for a short time. Liquid latex contains water. As the water evaporates, the individual rubber particles in the latex knit together and become solid rubber. The water needs to evaporate for the latex to form rubber. This means it is not possible to pour large amounts of latex over a model and have it cure. The latex exposed to air will form a skin, but the latex within the skin will stay liquid.

Latex moulded statue. Note the deep undercuts

You must use latex for mould making in thin layers. If you want a thicker mould, you must apply thin layers one at a time. Some drying time is necessary between each coat of latex.

Latex rubber reaches its full strength about a week after you have applied the last coat, at room temperature. You can speed the curing by putting the latex mould in a warm (200° F) oven. To keep the latex mould from losing its shape, you should leave it on your model while the latex cures.

If you use a latex mould before it has fully cured, you risk ripping, tearing, or distorting the rubber. To test a latex mould for a full cure, press the surface with a fingernail. If a mark shows, the rubber is not fully cured. If the rubber springs right back and no mark is visible, the rubber is cured.

Applying latex rubber

Latex rubber can be used to make very thin moulds, useful when the model has deep undercuts. The finished cured mould will have qualities approaching a rubber band as far as elasticity and strength. This type of mould is sometimes known as a skin mould.

You can apply further latex to your model with a brush, or by dipping the model into the rubber. This is important, latex must be applied in thin coats, thick coats will not cure.

If you use a brush with latex rubber without preparing the brush first, the rubber will quickly coagulate in the bristles and make the brush useless. To prepare your brush, mix about 1 teaspoon of liquid dish detergent in a cup of water. Immerse your brush in this and get it thoroughly wet. Whenever you are ready to apply liquid latex, shake or press out the brush on some newspapers or paper towels. Then dip in the latex and apply to your model. Keep your brush in the detergent solution between coats of latex. Clean the brush in the solution whenever needed while you are using the latex. When finished with a mould, wash your brush out with soap and water.

If latex does coagulate in your brush, you can clean it by soaking overnight in some naphtha, which can be bought as lighter fuel. Scrape the congealed latex out with a wire brush and wash the brush with soap and water.

Large model cast with latex mould

Fasten the model to a flat base. For small models, you can use a plastic lid from a food container. Apply the release agent to the model.

Prepare your brush, and apply a coat of latex to the model, as if you were painting it. Cover all the details in your model carefully with a thin coat. Do not let the latex form puddles at any low spots, keep the whole coat of latex the same thickness. Break any air bubbles in the latex.

Paint a circular area around the base of the model with latex. For small models, paint an area about 1" wide around the model. For larger models, paint a correspondingly larger area of the base. This part of your latex mould will serve two purposes. One, it forms a lip that will support the mould when you cast into it. And two, you will be able to see how thick your mould is, without disturbing the main part of the mould.

Beautifully cast resin model

Apply the first coat of latex. Do this carefully, avoiding air bubbles. Any imperfections in this surface will later show up in your cast product. When you first apply the latex, it will appear milky white. Let it dry until the latex looks translucent amber. This may take anywhere from a half hour to several hours depending on air temperature and air circulation. For faster drying, you can set up a fan, or direct a hair dryer on your model.

Apply additional coats of latex until your mould is the desired thickness. Let each coat dry until it is tacky, but not completely dry, before adding another. It is best not to allow more than 8 hours between coats, so that subsequent coats of latex stick to the previous coat. Apply each coat in a cross-hatched pattern. For example, apply the first coat in a vertical direction, the second coat in a horizontal direction, the third coat diagonally, and so on.

Suitable brushes for applying liquid latex

Continue until the mould is about 1/16 to 1/8 inch thick.

Allow the mould to cure while it is still on the model. Test to see if the rubber is cured by pressing a fingernail into the rubber. If the rubber springs right back without leaving a mark, the rubber is cured. If a mark stays in the rubber, let the mould cure longer. If necessary, make a plaster backup mould while the mould is still on the model. Small moulds up to about 6" in length will probably not need a mould box or backup mould.

Before you remove the mould from the model, dust the surface of the mould with talcum powder to stop the rubber sticking to itself. Strip the mould from the model by peeling or rolling it off. Dust inside the mould with Talcum Powder as you remove it.

Instead of brushing on coats of latex, you can dip your model into a container of latex and achieve the same result. The latex will form a thin layer with each dip. Let each layer dry to a tacky stage before applying another layer. Keep the container covered between dips.

Follow all the steps for brushing on the liquid latex, but dip the coats on rather than brush them on. Allow some latex to run down the model and collect on the base. After a few minutes, brush the pool of latex out to an even thickness. This forms a lip around the mould.

The major difference with the dipping method is that you have no control over the direction of the coats you put on. A mould made by the dipping method will be slightly weaker and more prone to tearing for this reason.

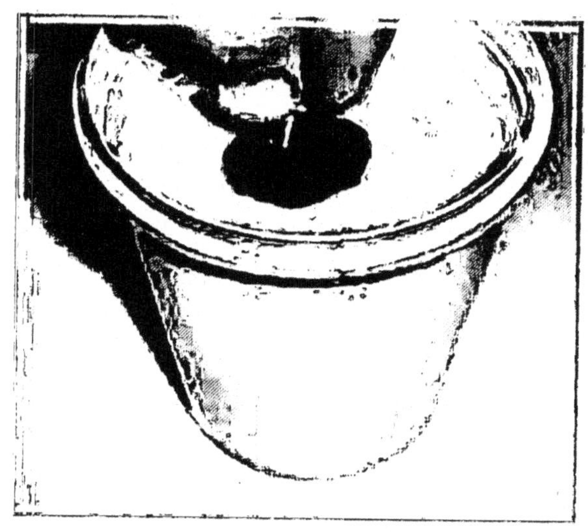

Dipping the model into liquid latex

Also, moulds made by the dipping method usually have a tackier surface than with the brush method. You must dust the outer surface of the mould with Talcum Powder (Baby Powder) before you remove the mould from your model. Dust the inside as you remove the mould.

After you apply the first two or three coats with the brush method, you can use Cheesecloth or Nylon Fabric as a reinforcing material. Simply embed the fabric or Cheesecloth strips in one or two layers of latex. Cheesecloth will prevent the latex from stretching, Nylon will allow the latex to stretch somewhat.

Think about how reinforcement will affect your ability to remove the mould. You are probably using moulding rubber for its ability to stretch and expand - any reinforcement will interfere with this. It is NOT usually necessary to use reinforcement - the rubber is strong all by itself.

A latex rubber mould will normally be quite thin and flexible. If you pour a casting material into a large latex rubber mould with no support, the mould may distort or sag out of shape. For this reason you may need to make what is known as a backup mould. A backup mould is simply a stiff mould around the latex mould. It holds the latex mould in position and provides support while casting into the latex mould. You can make backup moulds for latex rubber from plaster or fibreglass.

If you have moulded all sides of a model, your backup mould will need to be in two or more pieces. Though latex rubber can handle severe undercuts in a model, rigid mouldmaking materials cannot handle ANY undercuts. If the undercuts in the model are not severe, try to make your latex rubber mould with a smooth rounded outer surface. You can build up some parts of the latex as needed to eliminate undercuts.

If undercuts are severe and you cannot make the surface of the mould smooth and rounded with filler, you may need to make your plaster backup mould in more than two pieces. Each piece will remove in a different direction to avoid undercuts.

To make a backup mould from plaster, mix a batch of plaster with some reinforcement, such as chopped Burlap, The latex rubber mould should still be on the model. Paste the plaster on the part of the mould you are backing up in a layer about '/2 inch thick. Try to make the edge flat and even and the plaster a little thicker at the parting line. Let the plaster cure. Scrape the plaster as flat as possible at the parting line. Cut in some rounded depressions all along the parting line to serve as keys. Apply Petroleum Jelly (to the plaster only) as a release agent. Mix more plaster and reinforcement and cover the second half of the mould. Allow to cure, separate the halves, and peel off your rubber mould.

You may need filler for mouldmaking a large or complex mould, such as the garden frog above. If you need to have moulding rubber stay in place on a vertical surface of a model without running or sagging. And two, if your model needs a backup mould and has severe undercuts. Though rubber can handle undercuts by bending and stretching around them, a plaster backup mould cannot. You must make the surface of your rubber mould a smooth rounded shape so the plaster backup mould does not get trapped in any undercuts. You could use plain moulding rubber to build up the undercuts, but it might take many coats. The filled rubber lets you build up the areas much faster.

To use filler, add a small amount of the powder to a batch of moulding rubber, and mix thoroughly. Use the smallest amount that gives the results that you want. The more filler you use, the less elastic and more prone to tearing the mould will be. First, use several coats of moulding rubber on your model. Then use filled rubber to build up undercut areas. Use layers of about 1/8 inch, and let each layer dry. Then use more plain rubber to coat the filled rubber. This will result in the strongest moulds. You may find it easier to apply filled rubber with a spatula or craft stick, instead of a brush.

Latex rubber moulds will expand when soaked in naphtha or paraffin. This fact can be used to make enlargements of small objects by the following method:

Make a regular latex mould of a small object, such as one face and the edges of a coin. Do not use any reinforcement in the mould. Be sure to make a good size lip around the base of the mould. Allow the mould to cure completely.

If your model is damaged when you remove it from the mould, you may want to cast a reproduction now. After you expand the mould, the mould will be destroyed.

Immerse the entire mould in a container of naphtha or paraffin. The container should be large enough to allow the mould to double in size. The container should have a large enough opening so you can remove the expanded mould without bending it. Though latex rubber moulds are normally very strong, after you expand the mould it will be very weak and will tear easily. Every dimension of the mould will almost double in size after soaking for ten to twenty minutes. The mould will expand in length, width, and height or thickness. Do not let the mould soak for more time than necessary. After the mould has expanded, it will not get any bigger. It will only get weaker and more prone to tearing.

While the mould is still wet, use the mould to cast a reproduction. The expanded mould will shrink back to regular size if you allow it to dry out. Hang the expanded mould in a box the same way you would use a normal size mould. As soon as your casting material cures, you can remove your casting. The expanded mould will be destroyed, unless your original model was very simple, with no undercuts. Of course, you can make another mould of the casting if you wish. If your model had any complicated undercuts, the rubber may break off and remain in the undercut areas. Use tweezers if necessary to remove the rubber.

If you want to make even larger castings, you can make another latex mould of the first casting, and repeat the entire process. Similar to enlargements of photographs, each reproduction will be of somewhat lesser quality and detail than the previous ones. You can touch up the casting from each stage of the enlargement process before making the next latex mould.

As well as latex, there are many other materials that can be used to make moulds, all have their place in model making and their use will depend on the type of model to be moulded, as well as the casting material to be used. Acrylic rubber, for example, is the type of cheap water based material used for sealing gaps and cracks in window frames, and is found in tubes at most DIY stores. Acrylic sealants do provide a satisfactory flat impression of an object such as old coins etc. but are not ideal as they lack elasticity. They also take a long time to cure fully and shrink noticeably. They are very useful however as a "Fillet" material where joints have to be sealed, holes plugged etc. and not readily solvent when used in conjunction with most other non water based types. They are therefore ideal for this purpose because other rubbers will not stick directly to it.

Silicone rubbers are available in many types and from many different manufacturers. The mastic gun types are available out of tubes for sealing around bathtubs & window frames. Others are specialist RTV moulding silicones contain a separate curing agent or catalyst. The type most commonly used in mould making are in liquid form and the two pack variety are either weighed by ratio or measured 1:1, 2:1 etc. according to the manufacturer's instructions.

To achieve a "thinner" mix of the two, i.e... a more freely flowing medium; silicone oil may be added before use although this practice is usually applied to the thick tube type sealants but not exclusively as it does aid flow considerably.

Silicone based rubbers such as RTV are commonly used to produce superior reproductions of an object or plug as it will freely flow into the tiniest of cavities by gravity prior to curing under the correct conditions. These highly flexible rubbers have an extensive part to play amongst professional moulders. If quality casting is your aim then this should be your first choice as a moulding material as it will reproduce with remarkable detail from masters on average producing around 100 or more casts, it can also be used to cast in low melt metals such as pewter or lead.

Traditionally plaster of paris is used produce a support to hold the mould in position, or used to make the master from which you can make your reproductions. Larger quantities of plaster can be bought from most builders merchants. Plaster does not mix well with silicone unless it is primed and sealed first. If your master is made from plaster, you do not normally need to seal it if used with a latex mould as the water content from the latex will be absorbed into the plaster and will aid drying. If you prefer a smooth surface then it is advisable to seal your master first or use PVA mixed initially with the plaster before using. Also you should never allow plaster to come into contact with eyes or skin, especially lime based plasters which can cause serious burns.

Resins of all types are a very important material substance in the mould making industry and are used extensively for boat and ship building. They require the use of a catalyst to cure and can be reinforced with glass fibre rope, strand or matting.

There are many types of resins for use in filling flexible moulds including polyurethane and epoxy which are suitable. A resin cast can also be used as a more permanent plug. Subsequent moulds can then be taken from this.

Wax can be used for many different purposes in mould making including as filler for sealing around edges of containers which will take your mould. It can be used as a fill material by melting and pouring directly into the mould cavity, although this is not suitable for latex moulds. Another very good way of utilising this cheap material is to produce a block shape from which you can make carvings and/or a combination of melting certain parts with warm implements to achieve sculptured fine detail and smoothness.

Concrete can be used for filling to create a durable cast such as garden ornaments and robust furniture for use outdoors. Also as a two part sectional support for the mould to help retain shape when filled.

HEALTH & SAFETY NOTES:

- Do not inhale or ingest plaster powder.
- Large quantities of plaster can get extremely hot as it sets - UP TO 60C - DO NOT KEEP YOUR HANDS OR SKIN IN THE PLASTER AS IT SETS - clean your hands immediately after mixing.
- To clean your hands – wipe as much material off as you can, using disposable paper towels or even newspaper. Wash with lots of soap and lots and lots of water.
- If silicon or plaster gets splashed into eyes or hair, rinse immediately with plenty of cold water.

- If you have sensitive skin, use plastic gloves. A light coating of petroleum jelly or barrier cream will give a little bit of protection.
- Do not pour unused or used materials down the sinks.
- If using plastic sheeting – put newspaper on top to soak up any spills. Mop up any spills on the floor immediately and remember that wet floors (and wet plastic sheeting) are slippery.

CHAPTER 3

FURTHER MOULDMAKING

RTV, or room temperature vulcanising, is the material of choice for the serious modelmaker and resin caster. The use of RTV will result in a mould that is much tougher and more durable than the latex mould, although latex moulds can themselves be quite long lasting if made properly and looked after. However, for certain miniatures made from resin, the RTV mould will come to mind as the best solution.

Take for example the case of a military resin modeller. He may wish to produce (literally) legions of troops, whether for amateur, personal use or professional resale. RTV will allow a mould that very tough, a two part mould that can accommodate a large number of miniatures. In addition, these moulds lend themselves well to centrifugal casting, giving the best possible finish.

RTV Mould Aircraft Propeller

The mouldmaking process begins with the model, the pattern that you wish to duplicate. If it is made of porous materials such as plaster or wood, you will need to coat the model to seal the porosity of the pattern. If you are using a wax pattern or model made of a similarly impervious material, you not will not need release agents. If your model is made of plaster or wood, petroleum jelly or wax would be suitable as the release agent.

For making two part moulds, further release agent will be needed to coat the two surfaces of the mould that come into contact so that the mould will come apart after use.

When you have prepared your model, you need to mix the RTV compound according to the manufacturer's instructions. Carefully weigh out the two parts of the material. One part is a polysulfide rubber while the second is the catalyst. Use a clean metal, glass or plastic container to avoid contamination.

Mixing Bowl for RTV

It is important to mix gently to avoid entrapment of bubbles, if bubbles do appear, vacuum degassing may well be the only way to rid your mould of this problem. It is far better to mix very gently so as to avoid this problem from occurring at all.

Next you will pour or paint the curing RTV over the model. Work quickly as your activated moulding rubber only has a short 'open' life. After you have finished applying the RTV, let it stand for the manufacturer's recommended time to achieve maximum cure. Raising the temperature will speed up the cure, as will increased amounts of activator. However, it is best to avoid these measures unless time if absolutely critical. Speeding up the curing time can have an adverse effect on your mould.

If you wish to make a master model, perhaps you are considering a long production run, RTV may be used to make a master model. You must first make a negative mould out of plaster or a similar material. The RTV can then be poured into the negative mould. If you warm the mould first and tilt it, it will help to eliminate air bubbles. Some mould makers also brush in an initial coat RTV. If your model has a lot of undercuts, tilt the model to avoid air entrapment.

You should ensure that you store in a cool dry place without any distortion.

These are the general principles for making RTV moulds. Note the different types, the one piece mould for simple shapes and the two piece mould for more complex shapes.

If you are making a simple block mould, form a mould support around the master and pour the RTV rubber to cover the master and fill the mould support

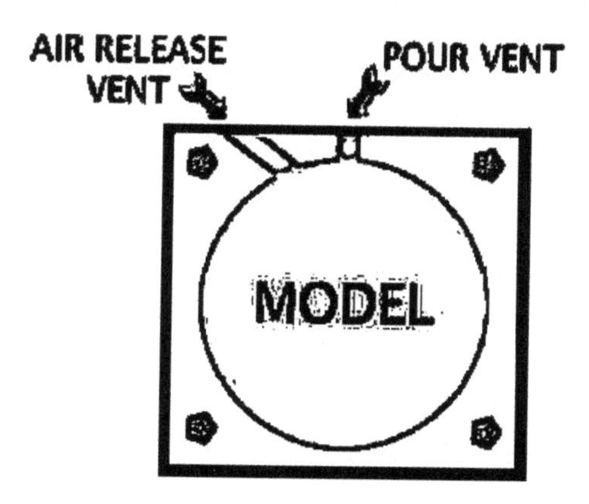

A support for a simple RTV mould

When the RTV silicone rubber cures, the bottom of the mould support is removed. A cover is placed over what had been the top of the support where the RTV silicone rubber had been poured in. The support is turned over and the master removed. This exposes the mould cavity for casting.

Glove moulds can be made in two different ways, either poured or laid up.

To prepare a glove mould, place a uniform layer of clay over the master making sure that your moulding material is compatible with the pattern material. Make a mould support from a material which will cure hard with a thin layer of clay at the base. Plaster or polyester with glass cloth reinforcement is frequently used for this purpose of mould supports. To allow for disassembly, the mould support can be made in two parts if necessary so that it can be dismantled two remove the mould when ready. The hardened mould support is removed and then the layer of clay is removed

The RTV silicone rubber is poured into this cavity and cured to form the mould and the master is removed to yield a finished mould.

Laid Up Glove Moulds

Laid up glove moulds do not give as uniform a thickness as poured glove moulds. They also may need to be cured in layers to get the desired thickness. However, the work of putting on and removing a layer of clay is saved. In addition, cloth reinforcement can be added to the mould more easily using this method.

The RTV silicone rubber can be applied with a spatula and/or stiff bristle brush. A jabbing motion with the brush may be required to make sure RTV silicone rubber gets into all areas. The master can now be removed to yield the finished mould. The finished mould looks similar to the poured glove mould.

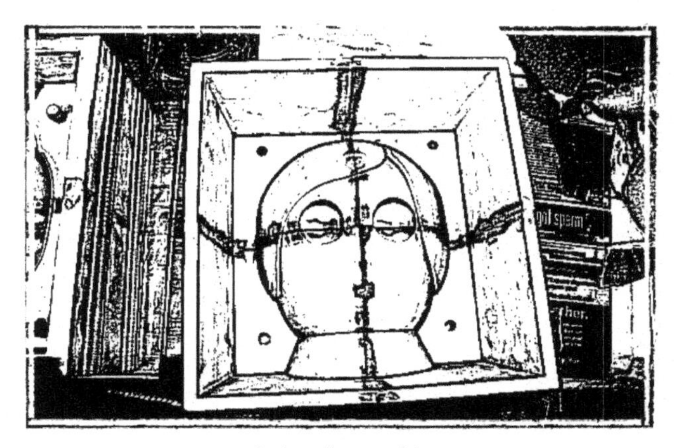

A simple mould

Often, due to part configuration, it is desirable to make a mould in two pieces rather than one; or, sometimes to cut a split into a one-piece mould to make part removal easier. This can be done with either block or glove moulds. In either case, careful consideration should be given to where the split is located on the part, as it will leave a parting line on it. Creating a split mould involves simply making a cut in the mould. During part removal, the mould can be opened at this split. Creating a two-piece mould involves several steps.

First, place the master within the mould support. Put a divider where the parting line is desired. A keyway built in at this divider will assure alignment of the two halves of the mould each time. Pour the first half of the RTV silicone rubber mould and allow it to cure.

Remove the divider. Apply a mould release on the exposed portions of the first half of the mould which will contact the second half to prevent the two mould halves from adhering together. Pour the second half of the RTV silicone rubber mould and allow it to cure. A cover is placed over what had been the top of the support where the RTV silicone rubber had been poured in. What had been the bottom is removed. This exposes the base of the master. The mould can be removed from the mould support the two halves can then be separated to remove the master. When reassembled without the master, the two halves form a finished mould.

Occasionally, a mould will tend to tear in a particular location. In these cases, it often is desirable to reinforce the mould with glass cloth. The glass cloth is actually built into the rubber. With poured moulds, this can be done by suspending the cloth above the master and pouring around it. With laid up moulds, usually a first layer of RTV silicone rubber is put on the master. Before this layer becomes tack free, the glass cloth is laid into it so that the silicone rubber soaks through. A second layer of RTV silicone rubber is then applied to make one integral mould. This procedure requires more labour, but gives increased resistance to tear.

RTV silicone rubber moulds are flexible. This is important for removing cast parts; however, to maintain proper dimensions of produced parts during the casting process, often it is necessary to build a rigid mould support structure around the silicone mould. This rigid mould support structure may be referred to by various names; e.g. mother mould, mould box, chase or surround. This mould support is usually, but not always, removed from the silicone rubber mould before removing cast parts. The mould support can be made of wood, metal, plaster, cast or fabricated plastic or a combination of these materials. Urethane, epoxy and glass-reinforced polyester are examples of plastics which can be used.

Sometimes the mould support is designed to fit quite close to the cast parts and conform to them, as is the case with a true glove mould. Other times the support is quite a bit larger than the part and doesn't follow the contours of the part at all. This would be the case with a true block mould. A hybrid is formed when a larger mould support has some pieces of wood or plastic, etc., used to fill some of the excess space. The space-filling pieces are called plugs.

For longer production moulding runs, spincasting is the preferred method. This involves making a circular mould. Spincasting is a method of casting using a centrifuge, as the circular mould spins around, the casting material is poured into a central hole in the mould. The centrifugal force forces the casting material to completely fill the mould, eliminating air pockets and other imperfections.

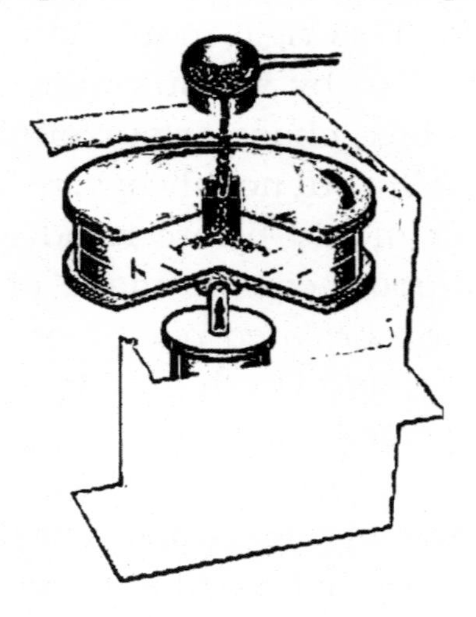

This method of casting uses a large rubber disc shaped mould, which is spun in the machine at high speed. This provides much more pressure than gravity casting, and consequently provides much more detail. There is no doubt that not only is this method of casting much quicker, but it is also the best way to cast your artefact and will give the best results. RTV rubber can be used to make spincast moulds. Spin casting uses centrifugal force to produce parts from a rubber mould. While spinning, casting material is poured into a mould, and centrifugal force pulls the material into the cavities. This accelerates production rates and preserves fine details for castings made of metal, plastic or wax.

In many ways, spin casting is similar to block mould RTV moulding. Both processes use rubber moulds that reproduce crisp details and accommodate undercuts. Additionally, spin casting RTV has some unique advantages over RTV block moulding. Because it uses organic or silicone rubber that is chemically cured, spin casting moulds can be ready for production in a short time. The properties of the rubber, combined with the spinning action, also result in extremely short cycle times. For some materials, parts are made in as little as 30 seconds. And a spin casting mould will usually have multiple cavities, so the short cycle time and multiple parts per cycle can yield fairly high production rates. Moulds are formed by placing patterns between shaped disks and adding RTV. The mould is then allowed to cure. When cured, the mould becomes firm yet flexible.

The mould is then loaded into a spin casting machine. After the spin cycle starts, the casting material is poured into the rotating mould. Pressure caused by centrifugal force pushes the liquid through the mould's runner system, completely filling each mould cavity. After the material has solidified, the mould is removed, and the castings are extracted.

Modern Spincasting machine

Typical spincasting moulds

Traditionally Plaster of Paris is used as the casting material available from hobby shops. Any type of plaster can be used in mould making and it is cheap to buy. Small quantities of finishing plaster can be bought from hobby or DIY stores mixed with PVA, and used as a material to produce a cast, a support to hold the mould in position, or used to make the master from which you can make your reproductions.

Larger quantities of plaster can be bought from most builders merchants. Plaster does not mix directly with silicone unless it is primed and sealed first. If your master is made from plaster, you do not normally need to seal it if used with a latex mould as the water content from the latex will be absorbed into the plaster and will aid drying. If you prefer a smooth surface then it is advisable to seal your master first or use PVA mixed initially with the plaster before using. Also you should never allow plaster to come into contact with eyes or skin, especially lime based plasters which can cause serious burns.Estimating the amount of rubber needed to make a mould can be a difficult task. However, having enough rubber or having too much rubber left over is not only frustrating, but costly. Successfully mastering this task is not that complicated and, like most things related to mould making, the more often you try it the better you become.

Well made RTV Mould

There are a number of variables to consider including complexity of the model (varying dimensions, configuration, undercuts, draft, etc.), type of mould being made (2 piece poured block vs. 3-D brush-on), type of mould rubber being used, etc.. The following will serve as a rudimentary way to mathematically estimate your material requirements for making moulds using rubber that is poured and rubber that is brushed on.

For moulds that are poured, we will assume that our model is a cube measuring 3" wide by 3" long and 3" high (7.62 cm X 7.62 cm X 7.62 cm). To hold both our model and the rubber, we will need a containment field or box that measures 4" wide, 4" long and 4" high (10.16cm X 10.16cm X 10.16cm).

The easiest way to estimate your rubber requirements (by volume) is to place the model in the containment field and pour water up and over the model. The amount of water used represents the amount of rubber you will need. Be careful to remove all water and thoroughly dry model and containment field before pouring rubber.

To estimate the amount of rubber needed by weight, we calculate the volume (cubic inches) of rubber needed to make the mould. This value, using the specific volume for the type of rubber used, will then be converted to mass or weight of rubber required.

Calculate volume of box holding the mould: 4" x 4" x 4" = 64 cubic inches (1,048.76 cubic centimetres).

Calculate volume of the cube: 3" x 3" x 3" = 27 cubic inches (442.45 cubic centimetres)

Subtract the volume of the cube from volume of the box to get total volume of rubber that you will need to make the mould: (B - A) = cubic inches to make mould. 64 cu. In. - 27 cu. In. = 37 cubic inches (1,048.76 - 442.45 = 606.31 cubic centimetres). 37 cubic inches (606.31 cm3) represents the volume of rubber needed to make the mould.

The next step is to convert the volume value (37 cu. in. or 606.31 cm3) to a weight value - pounds or kilos. To do this, you need to know what your mould rubber will yield on a cubic inches per pound (cm3/kilo) basis. The "value" you need to do this is called the "Specific Volume" and is included on most product technical bulletins

To calculate the weight, the next step is to divide the volume of the rubber needed to make the mould by the specific volume yield of the mould rubber.

If the intention is to make a brush on mould of the cube (used in our example above) by brushing a 14" (.65 cm.) layer of rubber over the entire surface area of the cube with the exception of the bottom of the cube that is resting on the table. The mould will be an open face mould with 5 sides of the cube covered with rubber.

Calculate surface area of cube that will be covered by rubber:

- Area of each side: 3" x 3" = 9 square inches (58.1 cm2)
- Total area: 5 sides x 9 sq. in. = 45 square inches (290.30 cm2).
- Calculate volume of rubber needed: Surface area of cube X thickness of brush on mould. 45 sq. in. x .25" = 11.25 cu. In. (184.4 cm3)
- Convert the volume value to a weight value -

pounds or kilos: 11.25 cu. In./19 cu. In per lb. = 0.59 lbs. 184.4 J 685 cm3.

Alginate is a useful mouldmaking material that produces a temporary but instant mould with a rubber like appearance.

To use alginate, shake the bag before use to loosen the powder.

Measuring by volume put equal parts of powder and cold clean water into a mixing bowl.

Working quickly, stir the mixture until it has a smooth and creamy consistency, avoid whipping and beating the mixture as this will create air bubbles which will ruin the finished mould.

Once thoroughly mixed there are two methods for producing the finished mould. For both you will need a container slightly bigger and deeper than the item to be copied. You can either:-

Pour the alginate mixture into the container and sink the object into the top making sure it is not completely immersed or place the object in the container and pour the alginate onto the top.

Once the alginate has been poured into the container tap the sides and base to encourage any air bubbles to rise to the surface. After approximately 4 minutes the texture of the alginate will resemble rubber and the object can either be lifted out or the mould can be peeled back.

Alginate cannot be used on porous objects or unglazed ceramics as it will stick to them and be impossible to remove. The moulds produced are temporary and should be cast from immediately. However, it is possible to prolong the life of a mould by storing it in a sealed plastic bag along with a damp cloth. This should keep the mould for approximately 48 hours.

As alginate sets so quickly, it is ideal for making moulds of hands/feet. Pour the mixed alginate into a bucket and submerge your hand making sure it does not come into contact with the sides of the bucket. Keep your hand still until the mould has set, then remove carefully. Pour in the plaster and leave to set. If it is impossible to remove the cast without damaging the mould, and you wish to use the mould again, follow the following instructions. Remove the mould from the container, cut it in half with a sharp scalpel and remove your cast. Put the mould back into the container making sure the two halves are tightly together and cast again.

TROUBLESHOOTING

Mould Rubber Did Not Cure At All

Wrong Mixing Proportions (Mix Ratio).
Did Not Use An Accurate Scale..

Room Temperature Too Cold.

Problem: partial cure (soft spots)

Not mixed thoroughly enough.
Not accurate enough in measuring
Did not "pre-mix" as directed by the technical bulletin.
Model was not properly prepared (resulting in contamination that inhibited the cure of the rubber.

Mould Rubber Stuck To My Model

Model Was Not Properly Sealed
Sealer was used or not enough was applied to the model.

Model Was Not Properly Released

Either the wrong release agent was applied, not enough was applied, or it was not applied properly.

IMPORTANT CONSIDERATIONS

- Whether you choose a, polyurethane or polysulfide, read the technical bulletin for that product. Every Smooth-On technical bulletin has important information about that specific product's use and technical information.

- Mouldmaking materials are safe if used properly and as directed.
- Mouldmaking and casting is not for children. Keep all materials out of the reach of children.
- Good ventilation is essential. You must use these products with at least room-size ventilation.
- Do not inhale fumes of rubber products, release agents, sealers, fillers, resins, plaster, etc.
- Wearing rubber gloves and long-sleeve garments will help minimize skin contact. If skin contact occurs, wash off immediately with soap and water. Uncured rubber can be removed from working surfaces with acetone.
- Be aware of your temperature. The workshop and all materials (including your mould) should be maintained at, or near, room temperature (77° F / 25°C). The colder the environment, the longer mould rubber will take to cure and if the temperature is too cold, (50°F / 10°C), the rubber will not cure at all. Warmer environments will reduce the amount of time you will have to mix and pour or brush on rubber.
- Humidity should also be kept at a minimum. High humidity will react with polyurethane mould rubbers.

TYPICAL MOULDS

Working surfaces should be accessible from at least two sides and should be level in all directions. To protect the surface from spills and stains, you may want to cover the tabletop with wax paper or brown wrapping paper. Also, if you are like most people, you will want to wear "disposable" clothing. These materials will permanently stain clothing.

Don't risk a valuable model, if you are unsure about compatibility between the mould rubber (sealer, release agent, etc.) and the model surface, test the material in question on a similar surface before applying to the model.

CHAPTER 4

CASTING

Once you have made your mould, using the most appropriate means for your project, the next step is to cast it. Resin casting is a process by which individual model parts can be copied and made repeatedly, for such as small production runs.

The advantages in being able to duplicate parts are many. You can make small as many copies of a particular model as you wish, or even produce them commercially. Resin casting is generally done by utilizing either a single or a two-part mould. The preparation of a two-part mould is somewhat more involved, but it does allow for the generation of full-bodied shapes in single pieces. The mould sections completely encase the pattern in question, and the resin is poured though an opening prepared at a strategic point. Upon curing, the mould halves are separated to reveal the completed part. Open face casting, utilizing a single mould, is a simpler and more common process and will be our primary subject of discussion. One allows for the fact that the top surface of the cast part will be unfinished, and will likely require sanding or other prep work upon extraction.

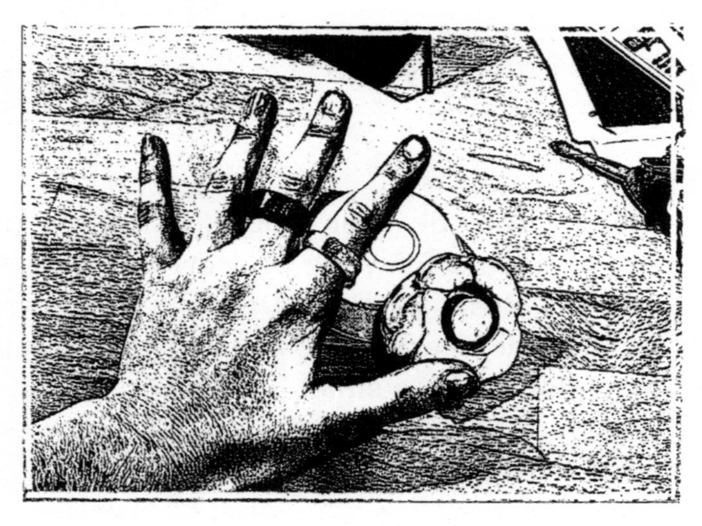

Resin Casting Rings

The process of open face casting requires a pattern with one flat surface which can be affixed to the bottom of a box or other containment dam, to make the mould. One then pours over the pattern a two-part liquid mixture of RTV, Room Temperature Vulcanizing, rubber. Curing time for the mould can be as quickly as overnight or even much quicker in some cases. If tight tolerances are required, however, it's a good idea to wait a few days before separating the pattern from the mould in order to achieve the smallest possible shrinkage factor. When the mould is freed from the pattern, it is ready to accept the resin pour, which is also a two-part catalyzed mixture. For small parts casting, there are a number of resins available, most with a fast cure time of approximately three minutes. If required, slower or faster curing resins can be obtained quite easily.

Shake both parts of your casting material first before you start to measure it. Pour both parts in equal amounts by volume into mixing container and stir, slowly and methodically. Be careful when mixing not to splash.

You only have 3 minutes from when you mix the two parts together before your resin starts to harden. For best results, pour the resin on a single spot at the lowest point of the containment field. The resin will seek its level and this should minimize air entrapment.

Time for removing the model form the mould will depend on the size of the part. Typically, with your 3 minute second resin time, you can remove within 5 to 10 minutes, although thin and fragile models will need much longer to cure hard.

Solid Casting means filling a mould completely with your casting material and allowing the material to cure. You can cast most materials except latex casting rubber and ceramic clay in solid blocks. Latex rubber will not cure in thick sections. Ceramic clay will shrink and crack. Also, you should not fire thick masses of ceramic clay in a kiln as they may explode because of trapped air.

Pouring pre-coloured resin

It is common to mix resin with various filler materials to make a solid cast product. You can use different fillers to give the finished product the look of metal, stone, wood, and so on. If you wish to make a material that resembles aluminium, the resin is normally mixed with powdered aluminium into the resin. A 50/50 mix by volume of aluminium to resin is quite common.

To put the metal in a plastic metal part, add powdered aluminium to the resin until the mix is the consistency of paste. Spoon or trowel this paste into your mould. Then bang the mould strongly on a table and the resin mix will settle down and fill the mould. The resulting cast part will be the equal of certain metal castings. After making a casting, the part will be a dull gray. Take some steel wool and rub the surface of the casting to make the metal shine. After this process the part will look like aluminium or pewter.

Aluminium is the most commonly used material for these castings because it is the least expensive. You also can use brass and bronze powders to give the effect of a cast metal art object, such as a bronze bust. Brass and Bronze powders are more expensive than aluminium, but can make some very attractive and realistic looking metal castings.

You can easily make very attractive coloured inlays in wood. Create your design by routing or drilling the wood. Mix resin with extra hardener and add the colour of your choice. Pour the resin into the design until the level of resin rises slightly above the surface of the surrounding wood. Allow the resin to cure for 24 hours. When the resin is hard, sand your inlay down flush with the surface of the wood. You can use ordinary sandpaper on a buffing wheel. A coat of varnish over the finished object will both protect and enhance it.

Making solid objects with hot melt vinyl is simply a matter of pouring the hot vinyl into a mould. You should fill your mould all at once with the hot vinyl. Filling a mould partially and then later filling it with more vinyl may result in a casting that comes apart during use.

The vinyl is very hot when you pour it - about 350° F. Be sure your mould will stand up to the heat, and will not leak or crack. Wear safety gloves and safety glasses when pouring the hot vinyl.

You can make thin-walled objects out of vinyl by dipping a shape (a Former) into hot vinyl. See the description of this process in the "Dip Casting" chapter of this Guide. This is how industry makes many commercial products, such as rubber boots that fit over electrical and mechanical joints in your car.

SLUSH CASTING

Another way of making a thin-walled or hollow product is to pour hot vinyl into a mould as usual, but before it cools completely, pour most of it back out. The vinyl that is next to the walls of the mould will cool first, and a layer of vinyl will stay in the mould. You can control the thickness of the wall by how long you let the vinyl sit in the mould.

Slush Casting is a casting technique used to make

thin-walled cast products. In general, you fill a mould with a casting material. The material next to the walls of the mould gels, hardens, or sets and you pour off the excess casting material. Different casting materials are slush cast using slightly different techniques.

Rotational Casting is a type of slush casting in which you put the casting material in a mould, and then rotate the mould in all directions. The casting material coats the entire inside surface of the mould. The result is a hollow cast product. Industrial manufacturers use rotational casting to produce items such as rubber balls, buckets, and tanks.

Slush cast model

If you plan to slush cast latex you will need a plaster mould. The plaster absorbs water from the liquid rubber. This causes the solid particles in the latex to knit together and form rubber next to the walls of the mould. Plaster is designed for absorbing water and will give best results.

There are several types of latex rubber. Latex rubber for “slush casting” or just “casting” is the type to get for this process. The moulds should NOT be bone dry. Dampen them by filling with water and letting them sit for 15 seconds or so before using. Damp moulds absorb water faster and more evenly than dry moulds. (Think about how you clean a spill off your kitchen counter - do you use a dry sponge or a damp sponge?) In latex rubber casting, the plaster mould is the “sponge” for absorbing water from the latex.

Have your moulds ready. Fasten two part moulds together with wire, string, or clamps.

Stir the latex thoroughly, stir the filler thoroughly, and measure the amounts you need of each into a separate container. Then mix them together thoroughly. You will need enough of the combined parts to fill your mould, with a little extra to top off the mould as the plaster withdraws water from the latex.

Making 2 part latex mould

SOLID CASTING PLASTER

Making solid cast products with Plaster is simply a matter of mixing the Plaster and pouring it into your mould. Remember that Plaster will cure to a rigid material, so if your moulds have undercuts, then the moulds must be flexible. About the only problem met when casting Plaster materials is small air bubbles, or "pin holes" in the surface of the cast product liquids known as Mould Releases or Mould Rinses are available to solve this problem. Fill the mould with mould rinse and pour back out. Or paint a coat of mould rinse onto the mould surface. Let the Mould Rinse dry, and then rinse the mould with water and pour your casting Plaster into the mould.

If 3 our mould is complicated, with undercuts and intricate details, put a small amount of Plaster into the mould first. Turn and tilt the mould so plaster coats all mould surfaces. Then pour the rest of the Plaster into the mould. If necessary, tilt the mould at an angle while you pour the Plaster so air can escape.

SPIN CASTING WITH RESIN

The mould is placed into the spincasting machine. Adjustments are made for table spin speed, cycle duration, and clamping pressure and the cycle is starting by simply closing the lid of the spin casting machine. Once the spincaster is up to speed, mix the resin as carefully and quickly as possible, the pour it into the funnel at the top of the machine. The centrifugal force created by the spinning of the casting table forces the resin into all of the cavities within the mould. The result is a perfectly cast part which retains all of the detail of the original model, right down to the surface texture.

Note that fast curing resins are not ideal for spin casting with resin. You will need a resin that is slower to cure to achieve the best results. Curing times can be slowed by using less catalyst, look at the manufacturer's technical data for guidance. With a little experience, you will get an idea of for the best material and mixture for any given situation.

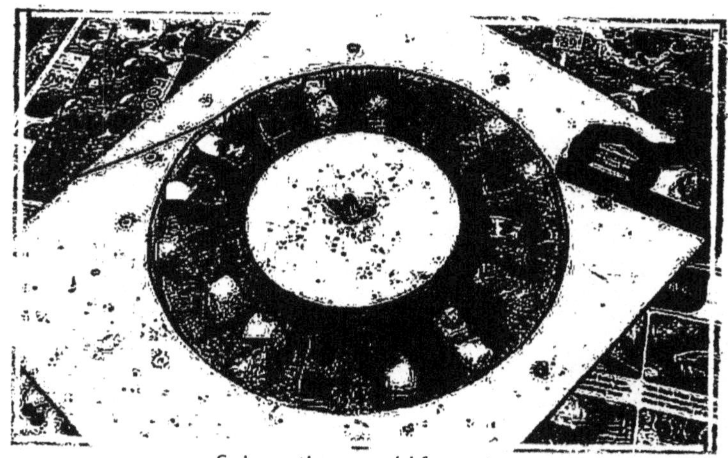

Spincasting mould for resin

Tomps in the UK do a polyurethane fast cast resin for casting and tooling. It has a 4-6 minute potlife and takes around 30 minutes to cure. It also has a very low viscosity, i.e. it is much thinner than conventional casting resin.

Tiny imperfections in cast surfaces are often caused by air bubbles in the resin mixture. Reducing the surface friction of the mould will force the tiny air pockets to rise to the surface of the pour, or away from away from what will eventually be the surface of the part. This is best accomplished by "dusting" the mould in question with standard talcum powder, then simply blowing it out before engaging the pour.

SPINCASTING

Spincasting is not a difficult technique to master, although it is more complicated and requires more care than simple casting from a basic single mould. The process is similar to normal casting, you apply mould release to both sides of the rubber mould, close the mould and place it in the spin casting machine. Then you add the casting material.

Putting the mould into the centrifugal casting machine

Choose an appropriate mould rubber based on your needs. Mould the first RTV disk and the models on the uncured rubber disc. Insert a centre plug into the middle of the rubber disc and arrange locknuts to ensure proper alignment of the two mould halves.

Place the rubber disc in a ring frame and dust with mica powder before mixing and adding the second mould half. Once the rubber mould has cured, remove your models from the mould frame set

Gates are now cut into the rubber mould to direct the resin into the model cavities during casting. In addition, vents are cut into the mould to prevent the build-up of gasses. The gates and vents are easily cut using a sharp knife and are specifically shaped to take advantage of the spin casting process.

Cutting gates and vents in the spin casting mould

With all of the gates and vents cut, the mould is placed into the spincasting machine. Adjustments are made for table spin speed, cycle duration, and clamping pressure and the cycle is starting by simply closing the lid of the spin casting machine. Molten metal is then poured into the funnel at the top of the machine. The centrifugal force created by the spinning of the casting table forces the molten metal into all of the cavities within the mould. The result is a perfectly cast part which retains all of the detail of the original model, right down to the surface texture.

LAMINATING

A technique of laminating can be used to make products from built up layers, or laminations of plastic resins and reinforcing materials. This will make a lighter product which is stronger and less expensive than if you had cast the product form solid resin. You also can make laminated sculptures and plaques from plaster. As a matter of interest, resin-impregnated polyester resin cloth or mat is laminated in layers to make fibreglass boat hulls, car bodies, motorcycle fairings, and many other products. For home use, you can use the process to make waterproof tanks and containers out of ordinary wooden boxes, repair rusted steel tanks, or make thin but strong moulds for casting other materials.

To make a lamination, mix up a batch of resin, and paint on to the mould you are laminating.

Before applying the resin to the mould, apply release agent so you can remove the lamination after the resin hardens. When the resin gets tacky, but before cure, press in a layer of fibreglass mat, apply more resin and press it in to the mat, so that the resin penetrates the mat and prevents any air bubbles. If you notice that any air bubbles have appeared, break them up immediately. Continue with layers of resin and fibreglass mat, until the lamination is as thick as you need. To build up more layers of lamination, not let the resin harden before adding more.

Laminating flat object with resin

Always add more glass mat and resin while the previous layer is still soft and tacky. If needed, add silica in small amounts to stiffen the mix. It will prevent the resin from running off, but still allow you to soak the fibreglass mat thoroughly.

Since you are using resin in thin layers, you will need to use more hardener than normal to get a quick cure fibreglass supply sources also have many other types of reinforcing materials similar to fibreglass mat. Some of them such as Kevlar fabric can make products that are stronger than steel, weight for weight. You can use these other reinforcements to make laminations the same way you use fibreglass mat. You can use polyester resin putties to make very strong and hard patches in wood, concrete, and metal.

To make a putty for repairing metal tanks, wooden boles, and so on you can use milled fibreglass, short fibre threads of glass. When added to the resin, they make a strong and tough putty material.

Add the milled fibreglass to the resin until the mix has a paste-like consistency. Use a putty knife to fill the area you are patching with the material. After curing, you can sand the patch to shape, and feather the edges, with files or sandpaper. If your patch is going to be thin, use more hardener than normal.

CHAPTER 5

VACUUM FORMING

Vacuum Forming or is a surprisingly simple process where a flat plastic sheet is heated until it's soft. Then you stretch it over a mould or pattern, and suck it down tightly with vacuum. The plastic cools quickly and retains that shape. Vacuum forming is ideal whenever you need a shell type plastic part with uniform wall thickness. You can form over wood, plaster and many other materials. A sheet of plastic is held in a clamping frame that grips it around the outside edges. This way it can be handled while it is soft. It is then moved close to a big heater, usually electric until it becomes soft and pliable.

An electric motor mounted on top of a large air tank drives a vacuum pump. It pumps as much air out of the tank as possible and actually works like an air compressor in reverse. When the plastic sheet is sufficiently soft and has the correct degree of sag, and all the air is pumped out of the tank, we are ready to form. The clamping frame then quickly lowers over the mould, and the hot plastic touches the edge of the vacuum box to form a seal. At this point the operator opens a large valve that is located between the tank and the vacuum box.

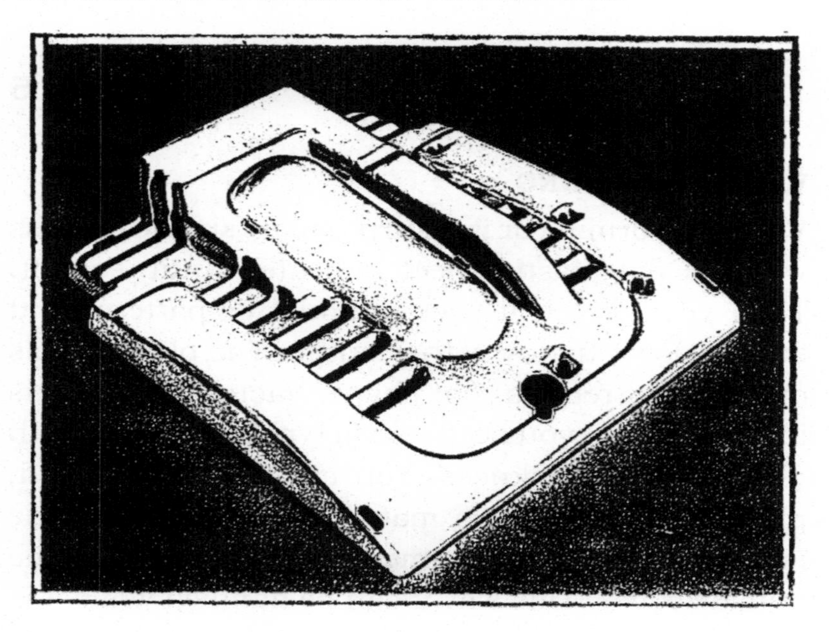

Typical Vacuum formed part

This causes all of the air under the sheet to rush in and try to fill the empty tank. This sucks the plastic down tightly to form the correct shape, and it is allowed to cool that way. When it is cool, the clamp frame can be lifted, the part is removed and replaced with a new flat sheet so the process can repeat itself.

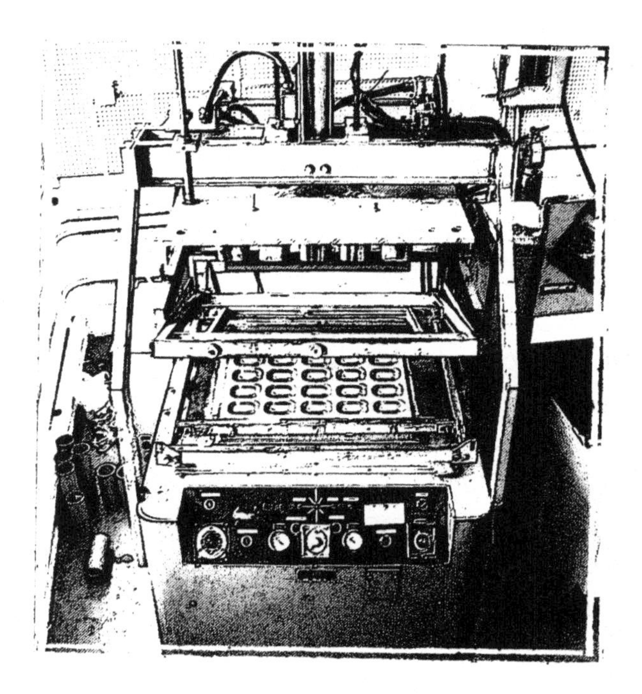

Vacuum forming machine

The large machine uses electric heaters that can heat up to more than 400°F. It also uses air tanks, pumps, motors and valves, etc., but the concept is still very simple. For smaller parts, up to about 10 x 18 inches, you can heat the plastic in your kitchen oven. This gets plenty hot enough, and probably has better heat control than the large industrial ovens. The large machines also use expensive pumps, motors and tanks to handle the vacuum. This is because they need to suck out much more air quickly enough to form the thick plastic before it cools. For smaller parts in thinner plastic, your home vacuum cleaner works pretty good, and it's not hard to obtain even more vacuum. Now all that is left is to make a simple frame to hold the plastic sheet, and a simple vacuum box from ordinary materials.

You can make model helicopter canopy, model off-road buggy panels (always needing replacement), and road car bodies. Model airplane canopies, wing tips, engine cowls, wheels and much more are just as easy. Model boat hulls and parts are equally simple, using the same process. These are all small parts in thin plastic that are ideal for making on a simple machine.

Basic Vacuum Forming Machine available on Amazon

Vacuum forming is ideal for making multiple parts cheaply. A simple wood or plaster mould can produce over 100 parts, and flat plastic sheets are fairly inexpensive. If you look around there are vacuum formed parts that you use or see every day, such as the inside of most refrigerators, luggage, signs, and a very common use is for packaging. The closest low cost alternative to vacuum forming that I could think of is fibreglass. If you think about it, fibreglass requires similar moulds, is more expensive for materials and takes much longer and more skill to use. Besides, it stinks and makes you itch! Then why is it so popular? It must be that the use of fibreglass is common knowledge, and little is known about vacuum forming. In fact, vacuum forming can be used to make fast and easy moulds to layup fibreglass parts. Simply form over an existing object and then use it as a female mould to make fibreglass duplicates.

To begin the moulding process, the operator sets a mould on the vacuum forming machine's mould table and clamps a plastic sheet into the machine's frame. An electric heater heats the plastic until it softens. The operator lowers the frame onto the mould, stretching the plastic so it conforms to the mould's shape. A vacuum pump draws air out from under the sheet, and it fits the mould exactly. When the plastic cools, the operator releases the moulded plastic piece from the machine.

Moulds can be made of many common materials, such as plastic, wood or metal, as long as they're stable and heat-resistant. Typical mould sizes range from a few inches to more than a foot. The size of the plastic sheet dictates the maximum mould size, and the mould designer must not create a mould so large or tall that the stretched sheet can't fit around it. If you're moulding small items, it makes sense to arrange several small moulds on the moulding table to make the most of every plastic sheet. The moulds must also have strategically placed vent holes so the air can be drawn out evenly, avoiding bubbles.

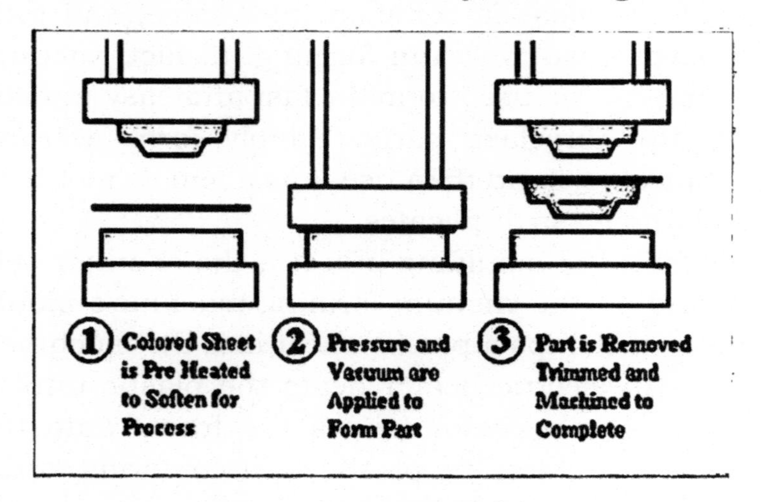

The vacuum forming process

The mould shapes have some limitations. For example, steeper draft angles, or angles measured from vertical, make the plastic more difficult to release from the mould. Angles under five degrees are not recommended. You must also avoid horizontal voids or dips into moulded shapes, as the mould would not release the plastic.

Vacuum forming machines use thermoplastic sheets, which means that the plastics soften when heated. They include polystyrene, acrylonitrile butadiene styrene (ABS), polyethylene terepthalate glycol (PETG) and acrylic. The sheet thickness is generally limited to under an eighth of an inch.

SAFETY WITH VACUUM FORMING

Forming temperature for most plastics is less than 400 degrees. At that temperature the plastic will get soft and droop, but that's all. It can stay that way for quite a while as long as you don't let it droop its way into contact with a heating element. There are many foods that will scorch and burn at lower temperatures than this. The nice thing is that ovens are designed for controlled heating and you can set them at a safe maximum temperature for the plastic you are using.

Common sense dictates that you never take your eyes off the plastic while it is heating, and you should open the windows if you smell any odour. At normal forming temperatures, most plastics give off little or no smell, but if you overheat them, they can produce smoke and toxic fumes. I think PVC is the worst. If you smell anything funny, turn off the oven, open the windows and leave the room until it clears.Vacuum cleaners are fairly safe as long as you don't trip over the cable, so you can be confident that vacuum forming is no more dangerous than cooking and cleaning.

HOW TO MAKE YOUR OWN VACUUM FORMER

The main parts to this machine are the top; which is the place that the object to be copied is put and the magic happens. This has holes drilled in it so the suction is about the same over the whole surface. -A hollow cavity, like a strong, airtight box. This is to get the same approximate suction on all parts of the top -A vacuum cleaner (shop vacs are a pretty ...

Drill lots of small holes in the lid of the jar, spaced about 1/4 of an inch apart. Try to evenly space them in a grid pattern. This will become the workspace. Second, cut a hole in the side of the peanut butter jar just large enough that little more than the tip of the 2 litre bottle top will fit through it.

Then use the knife to cut the top off of the coke bottle, Put the top of the bottle through the hole in the jar from the inside like this:

Make it Air Tight - now saran wrap and tape the whole assembly. (Make sure to get saran wrap in the threads of the screw top of the jar.)

Put the lid back on the jar. The whole thing should be air tight except for the holes in the top. For plastic, I use the sides of one-gallon water jugs or milk jugs. Cut off the sides of the jugs and clamp them (or hold them somehow) between the two frames.

Select whatever object you want to copy. Some tips on selecting objects: -- Make sure that the object is not tapered on the bottom. This will make it impossible to get out of the plastic shell we are making. -- Make sure that the entire object fits on the workspace leaving plenty of holes around the edges. --Make sure the object can stand the pressure and heat ...

Once the plastic is good and saggy, slowly place it over the object. The plastic will stretch over the object. Try to get a good seal all around the object, it should be air tight to get maximum suction. Once the airtight seal is formed, turn on the vacuum. Don't keep it on, just hit it with a good second-long burst. The plastic will suck tight to the object and the workspace. If when you turn off the vacuum cleaner, the plastic is still gooey enough to try to come up slightly, hit it again with another burst from the vacuum cleaner. It should be done by that point. Hold it steady as the plastic totally hardens. When it is done, leave it alone for a little while so the plastic cures. Cut the extra off and put it in the recycling bin and you are done!

GLOSSARY

Acrylic
A synthetic polymer used in resins and paints. Also used to make artificial teeth and dentures.

Airbrush
An atomizer for applying by compressed air a fine spray (as of paint or liquid colour). An airbrush is the best choice for painting masks and special effects props because of its ability to blend colours smoothly and naturally. We recommend an external mix brush such as the Paasche H for Mask Paint or the Iwata Revolution for fine detail work using FW Inks.

Alginate
A fast-setting mould material used to make casts from living people or delicate/ unstable/ perishable items. Dental Alginate is used to make casts of teeth and gums. Prosthetic Grade Cream Alginate is used

to make body part moulds.

Armature
A support for clay sculpture. For mask making and special make-up effects, a head form is used to support the clay and to ensure a proper fit for the finished mask or appliance.

Base Coat
Refers to the initial painting of an overall colour to a mask or prop. Subsequent colours are applied on top of the Base Coat.

Burlap
A strong, reinforcing fabric added to the outer layers of a plaster mould. Add strength and reduces the possibility of cracks forming in the mould. Burlap is sold by the yard.

Cast
An impression taken from an object with a liquid or plastic substance.

Casting
A material cast into a mould is referred to as a casting. A piece of sculpture is a good example of a casting. When casting a rubber mask, latex is poured and/or brushed into a rigid, plaster mould.

Castings can be made of either flexible or rigid materials. As a general rule of thumb, rigid casts are made from flexible moulds so they can be easily removed. Rigid casts are not generally made from rigid moulds as undercuts can cause the cast to lock into the mould.

Dividing Wall
A temporary wall made of water-based clay. Used to create a separation between the front and back halves of a mould.

Foam Latex
A special formulation of liquid latex rubber which is whipped with air and then baked into a sponge form. Used throughout the special effects industry for appliance make-up effects, prosthetics, costumes, and animatronics creatures, etc.

F/X
An abbreviation of "Effects". See Special Effects and SPFX.

Highlight
Highlights are painted to simulate where light would fall naturally on the high points of a mask or sculpture. This heightens a relief effect. Highlight paint can be made by lightening the base paint.

Kidney Tool
A flexible rubber palette used to direct the flow of plaster as it sets. If you want to make professional moulds, don't be caught without this tool.

Maquette
A small clay model created as a guide for a larger sculpture. A miniature full head armature is often used as a base for a mask maquette.

Mould
A reverse image negative cavity made from a three dimensional object. An example of this would be a mould made for a latex mask.

Mould Jacket
A rigid outer shell used to hold a flexible mould in place.

Mould-Making
The act or process of making moulds. Necessary for reproducing or transferring a three-dimensional pattern into a rigid or soft material.

Negative
The mould surface which contains a reverse three dimensional imprint of the positive sculpture. Moulds are classified as negatives.

Positive
Any sculpture or model used as a pattern for a negative mould.

Reference Material
Any visual information used as an aid in creating a sculpture, etc.

Resin
Any of a large class of synthetic products that have some of the physical properties of natural resins but are different chemically and used chiefly in plastics.

Shading
A painted-on shadow which is applied to recessed areas on masks and props to deepen a relief effect.

Silicone
An elastomer material used to make flexible rubber moulds.

Special Effects
A term used to describe special theatrical make-up effects, as well as other theatrical and film effects. Often abbreviated as SPFX or F/X.

Steel Palette
A piece of thin, flexible sheet metal which is used to

scrape a clay surface. Removes surface irregularities and helps in creating a smooth surface.

Surgical Adhesive
A strong non-toxic glue which has the ability to bind to human skin, such as Duo, used by the effects industry to attach Appliance Make-Up components.

Texture Stamp
A flexible stamp made from latex or flexible urethane. Texture Stamps are pressed onto a sculpture to impart texture and detail.

Ultra Cal
An industrial stone pattern material adapted from the tool and die industry. Used to create very hard, long lasting moulds.

Undercut
Any positive or negative area which creates a lock situation between the mould and casting. Undercuts are the main reason why mould makers usually select a soft mouldmaking compound such as silicone to cast rigid materials.

Lightning Source UK Ltd.
Milton Keynes UK
UKOW05f1945280617
304302UK00001B/69/P